HELLO SUCCESS

HOW COURAGEOUS LEADERS USE THEIR CORE GENIUS AND VOICES TO MAKE A POWERFUL IMPACT

CURATED BY

DR. IZDIHAR JAMIL, Ph.D.

FEATURING

BRENNA DAVIS
SELINA LÓPEZ HINOJOSA

HELLO SUCCESS

HOW COURAGEOUS LEADERS USE THEIR CORE GENIUS AND VOICES TO MAKE A POWERFUL IMPACT

Cover design by Dr. Izdihar Jamil, Ph.D.

Never Stop

Gotta have faith

Gotta be brave on the open road

Gotta be stronger than you've ever known

To carry those dreams

Gotta have love

Gotta be kind and patient with yourself

Gotta keep climbing over every hill

And crawl on your knees

Step into the great unknown

Go ahead and cross that bridge

Never stop, never pause

Take another little look in your heart

Never stop, never pause

Be the firework that you are

Born for the magic

Born for the magic

Born for the magic

Gotta be bold

In creating a world of possibilities

Gotta surrender to the Power beyond

And make the world smile

Gotta ask for help

Break those barriers down

The only time is now

Let your mind run wild

Step into the great unknown

Go ahead and cross that bridge

Never stop never pause

Take another little look in your heart

Never stop never pause

Be the firework that you are

Born for the magic

Born for the magic

Born for the magic

Born for the magic

Born for the magic

Born for the magic

Born for the magic

Written by Izdihar Jamil and Drew Lawrence

Music Composed by Drew Lawrence

6

Table of Contents

Introduction………………………………………8

Honor Your Plan…………………………...14

Harnessing the Power of Purpose to Drive

Success…………………………………..41

Rising up…………………………………...67

The 5-Step Action Plan……………………92

Introduction

My husband, Rizal says "I got my dream job. Do you want to move to America?". I left my family and a secure job at one of the top universities in Malaysia to move to Orange County, California. In coming to America, not only was I out of my comfort zone but also entered a world of uncertainty. I left everything that I know, thousands of miles away to support my husband with his dream job.

In 2019, I talked about success and wealth to a friend of mine, Bob, who owns a very successful vegan food company at an event in San Diego. What I realized was that my definition of success and wealth wasn't about me flying on a private jet to an exotic location, having millions of dollars in the bank, or even wearing designer clothes.

But rather my definition of success and wealth was something simpler - like having the freedom to stay home to raise my kids while running a business, choosing my working schedule, volunteering at my kids' school and being at their functions, cooking food for my family and having some money so I can have financial independence to buy things that I want.

It turns out that I am already living my own definition and success and just the simplicity of it shocked me. What I realized was that I get to create my own vision and standards of success that works for me and it doesn't have to be pretentious. Often, success is simpler than we think.

That's why I wanted to curate this book "Hello SUCCESS". I wanted to collaborate with two other courageous leaders - Brenna Davis and Selina López Hinojosa, who are creating their own pathway of success that's uniquely theirs. The best part is that they get to use their core genius and voices to make a bigger and more powerful impact on others.

Dr. Izdihar Jamil,Ph.D, an esteemed Visibility Expert and TEDxHuntingtonBeach Curator, fearlessly challenges the status quo and reveals her principles for embracing authenticity in the face of societal pressure. She empowers readers to find their own voice, honor their own standards and use it as a catalyst for change.

Brenna Davis, the visionary CEO of a multi-million

dollar company, leads by example, demonstrating

how one can achieve remarkable success without

compromising their core values. Her driving forces

and insights inspire readers to become impactful

leaders in their own right.

Selina López Hinojosa, the remarkable

Transformation Coach, shares her wisdom gained

from overcoming a gripping 20-year addiction. With

unwavering determination, she not only triumphs

over her personal struggles, but also unveils her secret

to maintaining a life of sobriety, offering hope to

those who seek a transformative path to recovery.

"Hello SUCCESS" is more than just a collection of inspiring stories. It's a practical guide that equips readers with actionable steps to trailblaze their own paths to success. Through practical steps, readers will discover how to unlock their true potential, leverage their unique talents, and make a lasting impact on the world.

What sets this book apart is its inclusion of real-life experiences from ordinary individuals who have made extraordinary decisions to challenge societal norms and forge their own definitions of success. These relatable stories serve as beacons of inspiration, reminding readers that they too have the power to overcome adversity and achieve greatness.

Prepare to be captivated by the transformative stories of these courageous leaders, as they show you how to tap into your core genius, find your voice, and make a powerful impact. Say HELLO to your personal journey of success as you embark on this remarkable exploration of resilience, authenticity, and the limitless possibilities that lie within you.

Here's to the unlimited POSSIBILITY of your own success,

Izdihar

Honor Your Plan

Dr. Izdihar Jamil, Ph.D.

Visibility Expert and TEDx Curator, USA

"Be brave in sharing your voice, stick to your plan and the opportunities will follow!"

- Dr. Izdihar Jamil

The Talk

My client Michelle said, "Izzy, you got to speak on the TEDx stage". It's been one of my dreams for many years but I said. "I just had a baby and I'm scared of public speaking. I don't think I can do this". Then Michelle said, "You're a trailblazer.

Where you go people follow. You want to create a path so other people can follow".

Many thoughts and emotions came through me. Can I really do it? How am I going to manage speaking on the TEDx stage and taking care of a baby? Public speaking just scares me- why do I even want to put myself through that torture?

Then I said, "Okay, let's do it". I applied to the first TEDx conference and the next one and the next one. Nine organizers said "NO" to me. I remembered picking up the phone to Michelle and just crying because when you get rejected from your dreams, it hurts.

There were times when I said to myself, "What's the point of doing this? It's just easier for me to give up". But then I woke up the next day preparing myself to apply to another conference until the perfect organizer, Sonali Fiske from TEDxDelthtroneWomen said "YES"!

My vision and Sonali's vision for TEDxDelthorneWomen couldn't have come at a better time or have been a better fit together. On December 4th, 2021, I gave my TEDx talk "Coming to America: A Story of A Hijab Wearing Woman" sharing my idea on how to overcome social adversity as an immigrant and hijab-wearing Muslim woman.

The Invite

When my TEDx talk was out, I was so excited that I shared it on my social media, my mailing list and sent personal messages to my friends about my talk. I shared my dream and my personal message to young girls and women about staying true to one's roots and heritage when faced with social adversity.

After a few months, I received a message from my friend Dr. Masni, who's a counselor at one of the top universities in Malaysia. She said, "I love your TEDx talk and I want you to come and speak at the university".

I couldn't believe it, Dr. Masni loves my talk and wants me to inspire the students at the university with my message. I said, "I would love to!". So I flew in from California to Malaysia to give the talk.

The 5-Minute Warning

On the day of the talk, Ayah drove me to the university - it was a 30-minute drive from my parent's place. I was catching up with Dr. Masni while she led me to the green room. It was so great seeing her again after so many years.

Five minutes before the talk started, the organizer said "By the way, the audience prefers and only likes speakers who speak in Malay or Arabic". At that moment, my jaw dropped and everything in me froze.

I'm a native Malay speaker and Malay is my first language. But to translate my entire three-hour talk from English to Malay in under five minutes is totally BONKERS! It isn't easy to translate everything from English to Malay despite being a native speaker.

Translating word for word would lead to a disaster because it may not convey the true meaning of the sentence and content. Translating a sentence from one language to another takes thoughtfulness, time and meticulous work to ensure that the meaning is not lost and the idea fully translated and understood.

I've spent my entire adult life presenting and speaking in English for my career and business.

I can't remember the last time that I had to present in Malay, probably when I was at elementary school and that was years ago.

What am I going to do?

I said to myself "Oh my God, they are not going to like me. They are going to ask me to leave". They are going to say "Look at her, she's a Malay and she's speaking in English. Now she's just showing off". I spent months preparing for the three-hour talk in English and now everything is about to crumble.

The Decision

One minute before the talk began, I had an intuition message that said "Just honor your plan and let your audience deal with you". What have I got to lose? I'll just honor my plan and give them the best talk because that's what I've practiced.

When the host says "Let's welcome to the stage our speaker, who comes all the way from California, Dr. Izdihar Jamil". As I entered the auditorium and looked at the faces of the audience, my heart was pumping up so fast and I felt a tingling sensation running through my body. I looked at a lady in the audience and I said my first line "I was at a grocery store getting some dates..."

Halfway through my talk, I decided that I wanted to make things slightly informal and I asked a question in Malay to the audience. One of the ladies in the audience raised her hand and gave her answer in English. Then a guy in the audience gave his point of view speaking in English too.

What just happened?

Here I am asking a question in Malay and the audience answered me in English. And this is after I was told that the audience prefers for the speaker to speak in either Malay or Arabic.

Not only that the audience dealt with me as is - a native Malay speaker who speaks in English but they also adapted to my preference of speaking in English.

Since then, I decided that I'll continue the rest of my talk in English and enjoy myself sharing my message and interacting with the audience.

The Invitation

That Friday after the talk, I received a call from one of the counselors from the University. She's one of Dr. Masni's colleagues. She said, "Assalamualaikum Dr. Iz. We would love for you to come and speak at the University next week. Are you available?".

I was speechless. I thought that speaking in English instead of Malay was the end of any further opportunities with the University.

Instead, it was an opening for another opportunity, by honoring my plan and letting the audience deal with me, I was being my true self and giving the audience the best talk I could give.

Imagine if I had chosen to translate the entire three-hour talk from English to Malay in less than five minutes, what would the experience be like for me and the audience? Will I be doing it justice or doing a disservice to the audience?

Honoring my plan allowed me to be at my highest potential. Rather than conforming to the external preconceived notion, I chose to be of service to giving my message and the audience the best experience and the best way to do that is by honoring my plan and letting the audience deal with me. When you stay true to that, opportunities will follow.

Key Lessons

Knowing what I know now, here are my top lessons
in how honoring your plan, despite society's
standards, can lead you to unexpected success.

Honor Your Plan

Changing your plan last minute can have a significant
impact, leading to increased anxiety and a lack of
solid structure to rely on. It disrupts the flow and
coherence of your work, potentially resulting in a
sloppy and unpolished outcome.

The sudden alteration can undermine confidence and
create a sense of uncertainty, affecting your ability to
execute tasks effectively.

It is important to carefully consider the implications of changing plans hastily, as it can have far-reaching consequences on productivity and the quality of your work.

Honoring your plan serves as a reflection of your thought process and demonstrates the value you place on commitment. By meticulously creating a plan, you invest time and care in crafting something special, tailored to your goals.

Following through with the plan allows you to perform at your most confident self, ensuring you give your best effort and maximize your chances of achieving the desired results. Honoring your plan signifies discipline, determination, and a strong commitment to personal growth.

Let The Audience Deal With You

Bo Eason was the first person that taught me the principle of "Let the audience deal with you". Often we think that we have to change ourselves, the way we speak, downplay our idea and change the way we look to please the audience.

But Bo taught me to come out to play as my best self and let the audience deal with me. You don't have to apologize for who you are. Be open, be vulnerable and hold the biggest vision that you have for the audience, a vision that is bigger than they have for themselves and you'll make yourself the most valuable player.

That's why I stuck to my plan and spoke in English despite the audience's preference for Malay or Arabic speakers. I let them deal with me showing up as my best version of myself- a talk that I have practiced for months.

I had the freedom to be who I am and because of that more opportunities followed.

Hold Your Standards

Holding to your standards is essential, as they reflect the principles that are non-negotiable to you. Amid societal pressures that may demand conformity, it becomes crucial to identify the standards you are 100% in alignment with.

These standards could encompass how you present yourself, your working hours, or the experience you want your audience or clients to have. Making a conscious decision to stand by your standards or conform to external demands is pivotal.

Straying from your standards can have a profound impact, potentially leading to a loss of authenticity, self-confidence, and trust from others. By upholding your standards, you maintain a sense of integrity and ensure that your actions and behaviors align with your core values, ultimately fostering personal growth and establishing meaningful connections.

One of my biggest standards is freedom and it's what I chose to operate in. For example, when I honored my plan and let the audience deal with me, I created freedom and space to fully express myself and the freedom for the audience to experience the unfiltered version of me.

Surrender

Surrendering what makes you great is a transformative decision, especially in a world where outside circumstances can unconsciously push us to do things that may not align with our true selves. Instead of striving for fame or trying to fit a mold, it is crucial to focus on the elements that make us unique and exceptional.

By surrendering to our inherent strengths, talents, and passions, we tap into our authentic power and purpose. Rather than seeking validation from others, we should prioritize being effective in delivering our message, making a meaningful impact, and staying true to our values.

Embracing what makes us great allows us to shine genuinely, cultivate fulfillment, and inspire others by exemplifying the power of authenticity. When I surrendered to my plan, I took bold and courageous actions to inspire others with my message at the university.

Your Essence

People are perceptive and have a keen ability to recognize authenticity. The audience is smart, able to see beyond superficial facades and recognize the essence of who you truly are. It is not the designer dress or the makeup that forges a genuine connection; it is the core of your being.

What truly resonates with them is your bravery, commitment, love, and generosity. When you reveal your true self, unafraid to be vulnerable and genuine, you create a profound connection with others.

They appreciate and value your authenticity over anything else.

By demonstrating your true essence, you invite others to do the same, fostering a deeper level of understanding, trust, and meaningful connections.

When you are in doubt or in a situation where you have to transform yourself to fit it, remember, be brave in sharing your voice, honor your plan and the opportunities will follow.

Power Summary

Let's review the key takeaways from this chapter:

1. Fill in the blanks. Honor the __________ and let the audience ______________.

2. What were my fears of speaking in English instead of in Malay?

3. Did I decide to speak in English or Malay?

   And   why?

☐

Success Actions

Here are three successful actions that you can do

today to be one step closer in making your dreams a

reality:

1. List one upcoming project/event that you are

   working on or are part of.

2. List one decision that you can make that will

   honor your plan for an upcoming

   event/project. For example, I decided to stick

   to my plan by speaking in English and letting

   the audience deal with me instead of speaking

   in Malay for the talk at the university.

3. List one outcome that can happen when you decide to honor your plan instead of conforming to the circumstances. For example, the audience spoke to me in English and I was invited to speak again.

Love and blessings,

Izdihar

"It takes COURAGE to share your voice so go and put more of yourself out there!" - Dr. Izdihar Jamil

About The Author

Dr. Izdihar Jamil, Ph.D., is an immigrant, Asian, hijab-wearing Muslim computer scientist turned visibility expert. She is a 17 times #1 International Bestselling Author of Are You Visible?, Women Who Lead, and Money Makers.

Izdihar has spoken at many prestigious events and interviews all around the world. She has her own TV Show called "It Takes COURAGE" where she features influential leaders discussing their success secrets. She was featured on FORBES, TED.com, FOX TV, NBC, CBS, ABC, CW, Thrive Global, and hundreds of media and publications.

In 2021, Izdihar was inducted into the prestigious Marquis Who's Who biography to recognize her contribution as one of the top 5% in the industry alongside Warren Buffet and Oprah.

Her TEDx Talk on overcoming social adversity and cultivating the courage to be proud of your roots and heritage has inspired many people from various cultures to take a positive step in accepting other people's principles and values.

She is an influential trailblazer and an inspirational leader in helping leaders to share their voices on prestigious platforms without prejudice.

She has helped hundreds of leaders to solidify their positions as the #1 Go-To Expert in their fields and get featured in major media and stages with her simple, no-fuss visibility methods.

Izdihar lives in California with her husband and three kids, and in her spare time, she loves reading and baking for her family.

More info: https://linktr.ee/izdiharjamil

Dedication

Thank you Abrar - for your commitment to your passion. Thank you Nadrah for the courage to be who you are. Thank you Rayhan for the joy and fun that you bring. Thank you Bee for the silent strength and unconditional support.

Praises for This Chapter

"Finally, a story that takes you from inspired to action in the best possible way! "

- **Erin Tran, 'My Yuko Journey Creator, United States**

"This read contains uplifting stories of resilience and staying true that force self-reflection for personal growth. Highly recommend it for anyone questioning their inner superpowers."

- **Jeremy Clark, Motivational Speaker, United States.**

"In a world where it can feel terrifying to be yourself, Izdihar's powerful storytelling and tangible lessons shows us that it's vital to your soul, your community, your business, and the world to trust and stay true to yourself."

- **Lisa Pezik, Off-Broadway Actor and Playwright, Messaging Strategist, TEDx Speaker, 2x Best Selling Author, Founder of Infinite Design House, Ontario Canada.**

Harnessing the Power of Purpose to Drive Success

By Brenna Davis, M.S.

CEO & Sustainable Business Expert

"Purpose helps us focus on more than just a monetary return – it encourages us to build a more equitable, sustainable and healthy world for future generations. That's true success."

– Brenna Davis

A Humble Start

My first teenage job was in a shabby, car-centric suburb of Seattle. I was working in a national chain drug store. After school, I stocked steel shelves with case after case of bandages, vitamins, ibuprofen, and those bright, cheap toys that distract kids while their parents shop. I rang people up at the register and attempted to make the right change. As a child, and teenager, I loved spending time in nature – gardening in my herb garden, running through the forest, or just watching plants and animals. This job was about as far away from what I loved as humanly possible.

The whole place was not fun. My co-workers and I moved through the long hours in a daze of carts and cardboard and occasionally helped elderly folks find the aspirin aisle.

 Most of my memories are of reading dot matrix

printer lists that dictated what merchandise went onto

which steel shelf. And then moving merchandise from

a cart to that place. I also remember that the 15-

minute breaks went by way too fast.

A pharmacy, though, is by definition, a place that

helps people. People go there for medicines that heal

and alleviate, and often show up at some of the most

vulnerable times in their lives. It's a jumping off

point for birthday parties with invitations, candy

colored wrapping paper and birthday cards. And it's

somewhere that you can help yourself get even more

gorgeous, where you can preserve your memories

with a print of a photograph, and or pick up a glossy

magazine that teaches you how to cook or remodel or

garden. A pharmacy is full of promise and purpose.

I didn't feel any of that purpose. I was a cog in a machine, a spoke in a wheel. I was a replenishment robot. No one talked to me or my co-workers about the pharmacy's purpose—the healing one, the one that mattered. And no one pointed out the nobility of the job—making people feel better.   My store manager was too focused on the numbers to inspire or even consider why we were there. So neither did we.

If my work at the pharmacy had been rooted in purpose – helping people get and stay healthy – I would have stayed longer. I would have felt inspired. I would have had a reason to place those countless boxes of cold medicines on the rack. I would have had a purpose for the work. And I would have been more successful.

The Train that Changed My Life

I was just sixteen when I worked at that pharmacy, so I didn't fully understand how purpose works or its full impact – what it means for growth and how it motivates and orients. Still, I longed to plug into something important and make a better world for everyone. I loved nature and felt called to protect the natural world. About a year and a half later, a fateful moment on a train changed my life.

At the time, my Mom was living in Los Angeles. She invited me down to visit, so I took the cheapest mode of travel - the train. I overstuffed a black duffle bag with way too many clothes and headed down to the grungy but still grand Union Station in Seattle.

As I boarded the train, I looked through the row of blue upholstered seats and found mine next to a gentleman in his late 50s. The train pulled from the station. We started to talk a bit and introduced ourselves. It turned out he was my friend's father! He also happened to be an environmental studies professor at Western Washington University. What were the odds?

As the 2-day long train ride unfolded, we talked more. I can tell you that when you sit next to someone for 37 hours, you learn a lot about them. We talked about politics, the environment, social issues, and so many more topics.

I shared my love of the environment and other issues. Toward the end of the train ride, he suggested that I consider a career in environmental studies.

In fact, he said he thought I would be great at it. It was the first time in my life someone told me that I would be good at a profession that engaged my passion for protecting the natural world – and it changed my life.

When I returned from Los Angeles, I enrolled in Shoreline Community College and started working towards a degree in environmental science. I worked in the field for more than 20 years, taking jobs in multiple industries and working on business sustainability before we even had a word for it. Later, I became the CEO of Organically Grown Company, a privately held, purpose trust-owned company that works to protect the health of people and the planet.

That train, that person, that conversation awakened me to the possibility that I could actually have a job grounded in my purpose.   And every day that I walk through the doors at my work, I connect with that purpose. I am successful at it for many reasons, but the biggest factor is that connection to purpose. It keeps me grounded, focused, and motivated.

PURPOSE POWER

We are living in an era of big change. Everything around us is shifting – the environment, the social landscape, and even what we eat. In a time when our new normal is disruption and crisis, we all need a way to float through the chaos.

Infusing our lives with our mission in life is a way to do just that. Purpose helps us to focus on more than just a monetary return – it encourages us to build a more equitable, sustainable, and healthy world for future generations. That's true success.

Purpose is often defined as your reason to be on the planet, or your mission in life. It's that inner urge to contribute to something larger than yourself. Or a feeling that this part of life is something you really want to improve.

True purpose comes in many shapes and sizes, but some examples are the drive to educate and mentor children, the desire to protect the planet for future generations, or the motivation to heal and share wisdom and experience with those less fortunate.

Whatever it is – you know you've found it inside yourself when you feel a drive and an urge to make it happen.

I am fortunate to have been working on sustainable business issues for two decades. I have also mentored and coached people from all over the country who want to embed purpose into their personal and professional lives. What I've learned is that when our work is focused on our mission in life, we are more content, centered, and fulfilled. Yet, many of us don't know what truly drives us or have our passions and true aims languish on the sidelines.

The reality is, every single one of us can embed our mission into one's day-to-day life without necessarily switching jobs.

We can easily work our purpose into our life no matter what, regardless of our job and position. Purpose can also be discovered in everyday tasks. When you're repairing something that's broken, chucking something into the recycling instead of the trash, making these things will give you a boost of purpose. Had I known this at the time, putting cases of bandages on the shelf at the pharmacy could have been a lot more meaningful for me---I only had to connect the work with helping people heal.

The truth is—now more than ever—we need people focused on purpose. In her diary, Ann Frank wrote: "How wonderful is it that nobody need to wait a single moment before starting to improve the world." We can all take small steps. The world needs us. And it is waiting for us to take action.

Finding your Purpose

Those I mentor and coach often feel disconnected from purpose. This is true of people in their 20s but also for some of those newly retired folks in their 60s. So, the question remains: How do you find purpose in your life?

A good first step is asking yourself a few questions, and then journaling the responses:

• What injustice do I see in the world that most hurts my heart?

• What am I most passionate about?

• What feels rewarding when I am doing it?

The process of considering these questions and writing down responses will identify an issue that is important to you. If you've located more than one, that's ok too many of us are frequently interested in a few different issues. Purpose can also shift over time. We are multifaceted people who shift, grow and change. And so do our priorities.

I used to dread any journaling prompt, so for those of you out there that experience the same feeling – I've got you. There are lots of other ways to access your inner purpose and wisdom. Let's check in with the heart to see what it tells us. Sit in a comfortable position, with your feet on the floor. Now, take a series of deep breaths, and place your hand on your heart.

Ask your heart what it knows about purpose. You might see a color or hear some words or even see an image that gives insight into your calling. If you don't sense anything, that's ok, too.

Another way to connect with purpose (especially for the deep thinkers) is to look back at who we were as children – how we skipped joyfully along, open to the world around us. One of my mentors, Char Sundust, says that you can look to your childhood to find your calling or purpose. What did you love doing as a child? What were you obsessed with?
Every child has her own unique gifts and talents. I loved spending time in nature, looking at plants, animals and insects. I also loved to garden and grew a lot of vegetables with my Dad. This led to a life closer to the earth.

As a result, I found my purpose in work that focused on healing the environment and helping people to get access to healthy, organic food.   What memories and experiences come to your forefront, what does that bring up for you?

Integrating Purpose into Your Life

Now that you've identified your mission or purpose, the next step is to take action. Integrating purpose into your life can be simple. You can accomplish it in lots of ways: bring it to your profession, infuse your workplace and home with it, or let it lead you in your volunteer work. And this is just the beginning—if maintained, it will permeate your life.

If you're like me, you may be in a profession that aligns with your purpose.

What if you aren't doing the job that is associated with your purpose? Maybe you don't want to be a doctor, but you care about children's health. In that case, you can find a way to turn your day-to-day life into your purpose. You can find a job working at a place that advances your life calling– like doing accounting in a local children's hospital. Another example that comes to mind is the truck drivers in my company. Many of them share that our company's mission inspires them. Knowing they help farmers and transport food that eventually winds up on family tables and plates gives them the boost they need to "keep on truckin'" as they say. When you apply your purpose to your skills, you change your inner dynamics, and this is a powerful way to drive success in both your life and your career.

Volunteering is also a rewarding path to integrating more purpose into your life. It's rewarding to spend time with people who care about the same issue that you do. And volunteering grows your circle of friends, which, in turn, brings you closer to the heart of your community. Research shows this is beneficial for your health and, really, how could it not be? I've found that the hardest part of volunteering is just showing up for your first event or meeting. After I "broke the seal" I found it easy to go back and see my new friends. Many websites, like VolunteerMatch, share opportunities by interest area. Just search for an opportunity related to your purpose! Remember that showing up the first time is sometimes the hardest part. You can do it.

Last, we can integrate purpose into our day-to-day

life simply by how we treat others. The simple acts

of treating others with kindness lead to actions that

are in harmony with a mission to change and heal the

world. It all starts by saying "Hi" to someone on the

street, cat-sitting for a neighbor, or helping an elderly

person with their groceries.

Caring for Yourself

I can't write about purpose and success without also

pointing out the importance of self-compassion.

Having a purpose is important, but we need to also

take care of ourselves. On an airplane, the flight

attendants instruct you to put your own life mask on

first. The Dalai Lama believes we must have

compassion for ourselves before we can have

compassion for others.

RuPaul Charles asks: "If you can't love yourself, how the hell are you gonna love someone else?" All three bits of sage advice remind us to prioritize our own well-being. Too often our purpose can override our own self-care, or we can pour so much of ourselves into it that we get burned out. So ask yourself, how am I taking care of myself? Am I sleeping, eating well, and moving my body enough? Is my inner dialogue kind? A good barometer for self-care is how we treat our best friend. Do we treat ourselves as well as our best friend? If not, we need to stop and readjust our priorities.

Key Lessons

#1 – Live your purpose—Success is more than just money. Without it, you're going through the motions in life, you are just like the teenage me, mindlessly putting products on the shelf. When you embed purpose into your life, you are happier, healthier and leave a positive legacy. It's like a love note to future generations. That is true success.

#2 Apply purpose to your life and work regardless of your profession. No matter what profession you are in. Whether you're a carpenter or a lawyer, you can find a way to engage your purpose. You can advance it through your day-to-day job in your organization or you can volunteer. Don't wait even one minute to apply yourself to your purpose.

#3 Care for yourself as much as your purpose.

Sometimes, you can focus on your purpose at the expense of our mental and physical health. Don't forget to take care of yourself. Make time and space for your self-care: it nurtures and replenishes you, giving you the energy required to advance your purpose. Just ask the Dalai Lama or Mama Ru.

Power Summary

Here is a recap of some of the major ideas from this chapter.

1. Fill in the blank. I think my purpose is

    __________________.

2. What will I do to work towards my purpose?

3. How am I taking care of myself as much as I

    care for my purpose?

Success Actions

Now that we have some ideas about purpose, here are some steps that you can personally take to understand and take action towards purposeful success.

1. Spend five minutes writing about your purpose. What is it? What about it drives you? Why do you care?

2. Write down one way that you will act on your purpose. For example, you might write that you will volunteer at a local beach cleanup. Or you might write down that you will start up a company that turns ocean plastic into a product.

3. Write down one thing that you will do to care for yourself as much as you do for your purpose. For example, you might decide to drink more water every day. Or you might decide to spend time with friends.

Wishing you beauty and light on your purpose

journey!

Brenna

About The Author

Brenna Davis, M.S. is a #1 international best-selling author, sustainable business expert, environmental scientist, and CEO of the first perpetual trust-owned company in the United States. An accomplished keynote and public speaker, her work has been featured on every major news network, including live morning television and on a panel facilitated by Vice President Al Gore.

She is the #1 International Bestselling Author of She's a Boss and contributed to Global Chorus: 365 Voices on the Future of the Planet. Brenna has mentored and coached hundreds of people around the country on purpose-driven careers. She lives in Portland, Oregon with her musician/artist husband and two opinionated and sweet rescue dogs.

More information about Brenna:

linktr.ee/thebrennaverse

Dedication: To Professor Ernst Gayden, who I met on that train. Thank you for inspiring me and connecting me with my purpose. I know you must still be helping to heal the Earth from heaven.

☐ Rising Up

By Selina López Hinojosa

CEO of LIFT by Selina & Transformation Coach

USA

"Once you make the decision that you want more out of life, you open the floodgates to endless possibilities." ~Selina López Hinojosa

Hidden by Shame

I grew up in Corpus Christi, Texas in a small barrio (a blue-collared, predominantly Hispanic neighborhood) called Los Encinos.

I was always a high achiever and was in gifted and talented education from kindergarten through high school. But when I was 16, I started partying. After my high school homecoming dance, a bunch of friends got together in a hotel room to drink. We each had our own bottle of Boone's Strawberry Hill Wine. "CHUG!" I drank that entire bottle all at once. It was the first time I ever got drunk, and I thought, "Why isn't everyone doing this all the time?!"

By my 20's, I was an alcoholic, smoking weed, popping pills, and snorting cocaine. Plus, I had a secret addiction: cutting. By this time, I was even married and had had my first son, Jay. You would think that this precious boy would've been my wake-up call.

However, one night, after swallowing two bottles of wine and several pills, I accidentally cut myself so deep that I was rushed to the ER, and I woke up in a psychiatric rehab facility. After 12 days, 1 was released, and relapsed shortly thereafter.

After grappling with the vicious cycle of addiction and all of the damaging effects it had on me, I went through a divorce and now needed a way to support myself and Jay. Somehow, I was able to pull myself together, although just enough, over the next couple of years and started working as a weight loss consultant at Jenny Craig. Then, I met Reggie. He was this cool, welder, biker, totally hot "Fix-It-Guy." We started hanging out and drinking with friends, and I assumed it was harmless, because I had convinced myself that I wasn't an addict anymore.

In 2015, Reggie and I had been married for a few years. I was blessed to have gained a stepson, Fabian, who was 14 at the time. Jay was now 12, and then we would go on to have Mossimo together, who was 6 at that time. Even though life was so good with my family, the weight of the depression was so heavy that I could feel the darkness in the depths of my soul. My favorite spot became this one single square cushion on our couch. Every morning I'd crawl out of bed, barely get the boys to school on time, come home, still in my pajamas, sit on that cushion with my bottle of wine, and cry most of the day. I'd be totally drunk by the time Reggie and the boys got home.

Feeling consumed and overwhelmed by the gravity of this addiction, coupled with chronic depression, I began preparing Reggie for the possibility that I would not survive this disease. "Babe, please take care of our boys when I'm gone," I would tell him. I'll never forget his desperate cries or the look on his face as he begged me not to leave them. It broke my heart, but I was completely helpless as the addiction and depression had such a choke hold on me.

Rising Up

Shortly thereafter, one afternoon, I was settled in with my wine when this picture of a Bible the boys brought home from church camp flashed in my mind. I hadn't held a Bible in years, but I got up and found it in a duffel bag under Jay's bed, brought it back to my cushion, started flipping through the pages, then randomly landed on Proverbs 23:31-32.

"Don't gaze at the wine, seeing how red it is, how it sparkles in the cup, how smoothly it goes down. In the end, it bites like a poisonous snake; it stings like a viper."

As I read these words, I felt a loving presence surrounding me, a complete warmth enveloped my entire being from the inside out. I knew, without a doubt, that I had changed forever! I felt an overwhelming sense of love and forgiveness; something different than anything I had ever experienced.

For the next six hours, I held tight to this feeling, and I was so excited when Reggie finally pulled into the driveway. I couldn't wait to share with him this transformational moment that I had. "Babe! I think I had an encounter with God! He wants me to follow Him."

It was then that Reggie saw a dramatic change in the

way I looked, the way I was talking, and even the

way I carried myself. It was undeniable to him that a

complete shift had taken place in me. He immediately

said, "I'll do it too, Babe. I'll follow God with you."

February 15th, 2015 was the last day I ever drank

alcohol or did drugs after 20 years of addiction.

Changing the Way I Think

Over the next year, all I focused on was my recovery. I started going to church consistently, studied scripture, and applied it to my daily life. This began my personal relationship with Jesus Christ as my Lord and Savior. I also received the proper mental health care that I desperately needed, and I started taking better care of my body with diet and exercise. All of these things began to work synergistically to improve my spiritual, emotional, mental, and physical health.

When I'd been sober for about a year, my mind and body felt healthy and strong again. The mental fog had lifted, and at last, I was thinking clearly. Soon after, we were finally able to afford our first home!

It had this old beat-up shed in the backyard. The moment I saw that shed, I thought, "This is where I'm going to start my new business!"

But then, I would hear this little voice inside my head saying, "Selina, you don't know ANYTHING about running a business. You don't even have any money. AND no one is gonna want to work out in your dirty shed anyway!" For the first time in a long time, I chose to ignore those negative thoughts. I now had the strength to change my thoughts into something good!

I decided to set up a bootcamp in the backyard and charge $5 per person. With a few pairs of dumbbells I had laying around, some cheap orange cones, and some Post-It notes, I designed my first outdoor circuit.

I texted friends and family saying, "Come for an awesome workout! Tomorrow at 6 pm!" The next day, 14 ladies showed up in my backyard! It was that day my business, LIFT by Selina, was born!

I discovered that as I changed the way that I thought, I started to view the world around me in a positive light, and I had more clarity for my future. I love what Romans 12:2 says, "Let God transform you into a new person by changing the way you think. Then you will learn God's will for you, which is good and pleasing and perfect."

Creating a Vision for the Life I Want

Since then, I have become a successful CEO and entrepreneur. Two years ago, I became the first Epic Fit Magazine cover model, and I've had two billboards in the middle of Times Square. I'll be giving a TEDx talk in Huntington Beach, CA in September, and I'm writing and recording my own songs! ME! …a former addict from the barrio with no college degree or business training!

My superpower is taking what I've learned from this journey to help hundreds of my clients overcome their barriers to reach their health, weight loss, and fitness goals. I coach my clients to adopt the behavioral patterns they need to achieve long-lasting results.

I tell all my clients, "If you do exactly what I tell you to do, I guarantee you'll get the results you want. The only way you won't be successful in my program is if you choose to give up."

I know all about wanting to give up, because I've lived it. The latter years of my addiction, I had just about given up on my life, because I truly thought that all I was ever going to be was a depressed, overweight, sloppy drunk. I now know that's exactly what the enemy was trying to convince me of in order to keep me stuck.

But once I began to visualize the woman God designed me to be, I had a picture in my mind of who she was. She was mentally strong, physically fit, confident, and successful.

I knew that I was going to have to take steps forward to become that woman; it wasn't just going to happen. I was ready to fight for the life I wanted for my family and me. Giving up would be the only thing that would stop me from becoming the woman I envisioned myself to be. By visualizing the life I wanted and working consistently towards it, I began creating a new reality for myself based on the truth of God's Word. The Bible says, in Jeremiah 29:11, "For I know the plans I have for you," says the Lord. "They are plans for good, and not for disaster, to give you a future, and a hope."

How to Quit Giving up on Your Dreams

I've come to realize that there are 3 reasons people give up on pursuing their dreams. Learn how to avoid or overcome these emotions:

Exhaustion- Long-term exhaustion, usually caused by stress, will eventually lead to burnout. Stress makes us exhausted, and without some kind of intervention, you're likely to give up. Taking care of your mind and body is essential to staying healthy, strong, and energized.

Discouragement- It's easy to veer off track with your goals from time to time, and sometimes, it can seem impossible to get back on track. When this happens, you have only two choices; you can give up, or you can CHOOSE to pick yourself up and keep going.

For additional moral support, I highly recommend finding a mentor or hiring a coach to help keep you accountable, encouraged, and focused.

Pride- The pursuit of your dreams will come with many challenges, and there will be times that you fail some of those challenges. Rather than working harder or trying a different approach, pride will deceive you into giving up altogether. Pride is extremely detrimental to your overall well-being. One way to avoid pride is to remain humble so that you can see yourself and your actions accurately. This will give you an open heart that is receptive to learning and receiving wisdom.

Key Lessons

Here are the top 3 things you can do for positive change in your life:

#1- Change the way you think. Doubts will creep into your mind from time to time. You'll have to dig deep down inside yourself to overcome thoughts of giving up. Push forward with all the strength you have, because your life and your future depend on it. Ignore those doubtful thoughts and keep going. Tune out any outside voices that don't support your dreams, and pay attention to your inner voice.

#2- Envision the life you want. Envision the strong, successful person you know you're meant to be. What does that person's life look like? What kind of things does that person do, or doesn't do, every single day to make them great? Consider making a vision board with pictures and words that inspire you and that represent the person you're aiming to become. Start behaving like that person today!

#3- Quit giving up. The three reasons people give up on their dreams are exhaustion, discouragement, and pride. Avoiding and/or overcoming them will be an important factor to pursuing your dreams.

Always be alert if any of these emotions are affecting you, because if they go unchecked, each one of them can cause you to give up on your deepest aspirations. Surround yourself with friends, family, mentors, and coaches who will encourage you to live a positive and healthy lifestyle.

Power Summary

Let's review the key lessons from this chapter.

1. What did I discover that helped me view the world in a more positive light?

2. What is the one thing I tell all my clients?

3. The three main reasons people give up on
their dreams are _______________,
_______________, and _______________.

Success Actions

Take these three steps toward pursuing your dreams:

1. Determine your ultimate goal and write it
down. For example, where would you like to
see yourself in a year?

2. Next, identify ONE behavior or activity that
you will start doing today that will get you
closer to that goal; one that you can manage.

3. Then, choose ONE behavior or activity that you are not going to do anymore; one that may be hindering your success.

"What you choose to do today can change the whole trajectory of your life."

~Selina López Hinojosa

Choose to change!

☐

About The Author

Selina López Hinojosa is the CEO of LIFT by Selina-

Health & Fitness Center, in Corpus Christi, TX where

she practices as a Master Fitness Trainer and

Transformation Coach.

She has been a guest on several podcasts including

Leading Ladies of Corpus Christi, Corpus Christi

Influencers, and The Monica Brant Show.

Her story has been in media publications such as Telemundo, Subkit Solopreneurs, and Bodyscape Magazine. In February of 2021, Selina graced the cover of the first issue of Epic Fit Magazine and was featured on two Supermodels Unlimited billboards in Times Square.

Selina completed Bo Eason's year-long Warrior Mastermind program to learn how to effectively share her story on stage. She is also a professionally trained singer, and songwriter and is currently working with multi-platinum singer/songwriter, Drew Lawrence, to write and record her own songs. She will be a featured speaker at TEDx Huntington Beach, CA in September 2023, curated by Dr. Izdihar Jamil.

Selina resides in Corpus Christi, Texas with her husband, Reggie, and three sons; Fabian- 24, Jay- 20, and Mossimo- 14.

https://linktr.ee/liftbyselina

Dedication

To my son Mossimo, thank you for always being my #1 cheerleader. Your encouragement means the world to me. You're the BEST!

Praises for the chapter

"This chapter is but a mere glimpse into the miraculous life-changing events that Selina López Hinojosa encountered in her life. While reading this, you will get a brief overview of how she was able to go from almost losing her life to connecting to God and re-calibrating into a STRONG woman of COURAGE, FAITH, HEALTH and FITNESS! She's been able to help thousands of others through her message of hope and her fitness programs. You will walk away inspired with courage and even action steps for doing the same thing in your own life -- so powerful!" - Monica Braslau, Monica Braslau Life Coaching, USA

The 5-Step Action Plan

We wanted to leave you with something tangible that you can take away from this chapter, like a mini-coaching strategy session from us. So we have combined our wisdom and curated "The Five Action Steps" chapter, providing you with a practical and actionable guide that will empower you to make a bigger impact and trailblaze your path to success. Each step is designed to help you discover your passion, embrace your ultimate dream, identify your standards, eliminate distractions, and foster accountability and alignment. Get ready to embark on a transformative journey as we guide you through these essential actions.

Step 01: Discover Your Passion

A life anchored in purpose is a life well-led. We want you to explore the importance of discovering your passion and aligning your work with your life's purpose. By centering your efforts around what truly drives you, you will find yourself more content, centered, and fulfilled. Uncover the core of your passion and embrace it as the fuel that will propel you toward making a powerful impact.

Step 02: Ultimate Dream

It's time to dream big and write down your ONE ultimate dream for this year. This goal should scare you and push you beyond your comfort zone. Embracing audacious dreams, that challenge you to grow, evolve, and reach heights you never thought possible.

By clearly defining and committing to this ultimate dream, you set the stage for an extraordinary journey of self-discovery and achievement.

Step 03: Identify Your Standards

To achieve your ultimate dream, it is essential to identify your non-negotiable standards. These standards serve as guiding principles that you will honor, regardless of the challenges you may face along the way. For example, Dr. Izdihar Jamil's standard, "Honor your plan and let the audience deal with you," reminds us to stay true to ourselves and trust in our vision, even when others may doubt or question us.

Step 04: Elimination

Simplicity is key to success. We encourage you to identify one thing or person that may be a distraction or potentially hinder your progress. By eliminating this distraction, you create space for focused action and enable yourself to concentrate on what truly matters. Keep your attention on the essentials and watch as your path to success becomes clearer and more attainable.

Step 05: Accountability and Alignment

Accountability and alignment are powerful forces on the journey to success. Find a trusted partner who will hold you accountable to your dreams and help you stay in alignment with your purpose.

This person should understand your vision, share your values, and provide support and guidance when needed. Together, you will create a dynamic partnership that propels you forward, even in the face of obstacles.

With "The 5-Step Action Plan" in your arsenal, you have a practical, step-by-step guide to make a profound impact and trailblaze your path to success. Discover your passion, embrace audacious dreams, uphold your non-negotiable standards, eliminate distractions, and find an accountability partner who will walk alongside you on this transformative journey. Get ready to unleash your core genius, amplify your voice, and create a powerful impact that leaves a legacy to make the world smile.

To leaving an impactful legacy,

Izdihar, Brenna and Selina